Vermont
TRAVEL JOURNAL

Souvenir

EDITED BY SANDY LEVESQUE

GILEAD HOUSE PUBLISHING

RANDOLPH, VERMONT

Editor: Sandy Levesque
sandy@sandylevesque.com

GILEAD HOUSE PUBLISHING
100 Gilead Brook Road
Randolph, Vermont 05060

Designed by Ann Aspell

Vintage Postcard Collections of Sandy Levesque and
the Vermont Historical Society

Vermont map courtesy of The Vermont Center for Geographic Information

Printed by Braintree Printing Inc. in Braintree, Massachusetts
Fourth Edition, February 2020

ISBN Number: 978-1-4675-9824-8

THIS JOURNAL BELONGS TO

_____

INTRODUCTION
Vermont's 255 Places

BEAUTIFUL IS THE WORD MOST OFTEN USED TO DESCRIBE VERMONT, a rural state of postcard vistas and a human scale that invites exploration. While it is possible to drive its length in less than four hours and its width in half that time, a departure from Vermont's highways to its back roads will reveal a succession of hidden beauties and startling seasonal landscapes that are yours to define in the pages of this journal.

Much of the aptly named Green Mountain state is composed of small but lively towns of one to five thousand people with even smaller villages and settlements sized just right to build strong communities. Vermont's total landmass of 9,165 square miles is divided into 255 civic/geographic entities or "places" that include 9 cities, 237 towns, 5 unorganized towns, 3 gores and one grant. All 255 are listed with their grant, charter, or patent date in this journal.

In the years following the French and Indian Wars, as southern New England became overpopulated and the region's agricultural lands exhausted, attention turned to the "northern frontier," a forested wilderness that would become Vermont. Between 1750 and 1799 most of the state was settled from south to north, first to the west of the Green Mountains and then to the east, with land grants from New Hampshire, patents for town-sized tracts of land from New York, and charters for parcels of land from Vermont. The independent Republic of Vermont, established in 1777, became the fourteenth member of the United States of America in 1791.

Today Vermont has 237 "organized/incorporated" towns, each with its own local government. It also has five "unorganized/unincorporated" towns granted by New Hampshire in 1761 and 1762 that have few or no permanent residents. In the southern part of the state Glastenbury and Somerset were once organized towns with local governments but so few citizens that they were disenfranchised by the Vermont legislature in 1937. In Essex County, on the northeastern side of the state, the New Hampshire grants of Averill and

Ferdinand never had a large enough population to be organized into towns and densely forested Lewis has yet to attract a settler.

Vermont's three official gores, Averys Gore, Buels Gore, and Warren Gore, are small irregularly shaped scraps of land that were leftover or overlooked when grants for square towns (usually six miles by six miles) were surveyed and mapped. They are all that remain of the bits and pieces of unclaimed territory wedged in between land grants, drawing their name from the triangular pieces of material used to widen or change the shape of a sail, skirt, or glove. Dozens of other gores were annexed to one or more adjacent towns.

Warners Grant is a remote stretch of land — 2,000 acres in Orleans County given to the widow (Hester) and three children of Revolutionary War hero General Seth Warner by an act of the Vermont legislature in 1791. Then, as now, Warners Grant is a wild terrain on which nobody wishes to live.

Vermont's nine cities vary in size from its smallest, Vergennes, the third oldest incorporated city in the United States with approximately 2,500 citizens, to Burlington, the state's biggest city of 42,000. The other places incorporated as municipalities are Barre, Montpelier, Newport, Rutland, St. Albans, South Burlington, and Winooski.

When your travel curiosity takes you to one of these cities, it won't be long before you find yourself on another back road scanning for a hand-hewn barn, a secret swimming hole, a covered bridge, a blazing autumn hillside, or the soaring church spire that promises a village just ahead.

This travel journal, with its alphabetical listing of Vermont's cities, towns, gores and grant, encourages you to record a favorite memory from each of the 255 places. Or you may decide to simply validate your visit in the allotted space. In either case, when the road comes to an end, whether in days or a lifetime, you will have created a unique, personal keepsake of a time and your place in Vermont's story.

The joy — and the beauty — are in the journey. Enjoy.

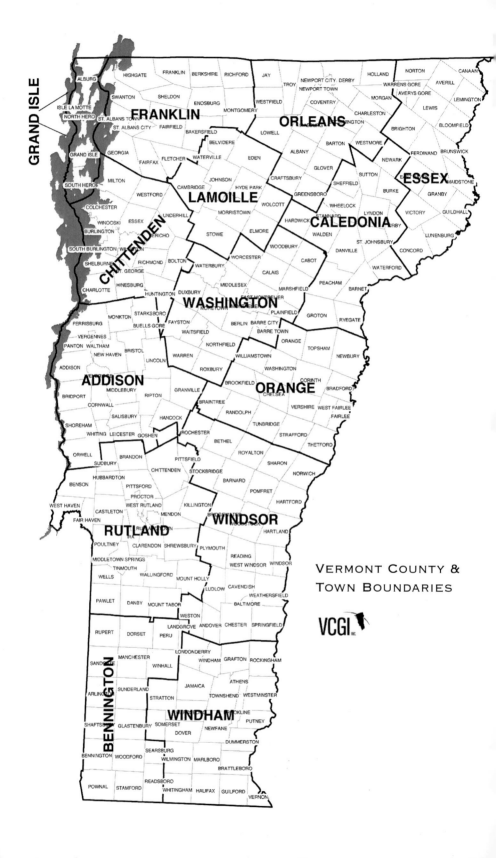

VERMONT COUNTY &
TOWN BOUNDARIES

VCGI

THE IDEA OF ESTABLISHING A CLUB TO ENCOURAGE VISITS TO ALL of Vermont's 251 towns and cities (255 places minus the state's three gores and one grant), was suggested 66 years ago by Dr. Arthur W. Peach in "At the Sign of the Quill," the popular literary column he wrote for *Vermont Life Magazine.*

A poet, professor, writer, and historian, effusive about all things Vermont, Dr. Peach was introduced to *Vermont Life* readers in 1947 as an Editorial Associate and the "man who has come to stand for Vermont to those who read about her both inside and outside her boundaries."

Since 1954, an organization of Vermont enthusiasts whose objective is to visit the state's 251 towns and cities.

He proposed a 251 Club in response to countless readers asking, "How can I come to know the real Vermont?"

Dr. Peach was committed to the idea that every corner of his home state had attractions, beauty, history, traditions and people of interest. In the Summer 1954 issue he invited "the native born and those born elsewhere but with Vermont in them" to veer from the beaten path "to discover the secret and lovely places that main roads do not reveal." Given the magazine's wide circulation the response from within and outside of Vermont's borders was remarkable.

Six decades later, interest in knowing the real Vermont remains strong as over 5,000 members of the 251 Club adventure through the state inspired by Dr. Peach,

"A swift turn from one of our main roads, and you are on your way to the rewarding experience of a lifetime and memories good until the years are frosty."

Dr. Peach's ideas about how the club should operate remain virtually unchanged. Members are encouraged to travel at their own pace, by car, on foot, or whatever conveyance suits their style. There are no membership requirements. There are no rules. There are no records to keep although many members document their travels with photographs, journals, or blogs.

A welcome addition that Dr. Peach could not have imagined in 1954 is the 251 Club's comprehensive web site, vt251.com, that you are invited to visit as you begin your exploration of all that Vermont has to offer.

VERMONT TRAVEL RESOURCES

MAPS

The Vermont Atlas & Gazetteer, published by DeLorme
Vermont Road Atlas, published by JIMAPCO
Vermont Road Atlas & Guide, published by Northern Cartographic

BOOKS

An Explorer's Guide Vermont (Thirteenth Edition), by Christina Tree and
    Rachel Carter
Country Stores of Vermont: A History and Guide, by Dennis Bathory-Kitsz
Covered Bridges of Vermont, by Ed Barna
Crossings: A History of Vermont Bridges, by Robert McCullough
Day Hiker's Guide to Vermont: Exploring the Green Mountain State, by the Green
    Mountain Club
Discover Vermont: The Vermont Life Guide to Exploring Our Rural Landscape,
    by Mark Bushnell
Field Guide to New England Barns and Farm Buildings, Thomas Durant Visser
Freedom and Unity: A History of Vermont, by Michael Sherman, Gene Sessions and
    P. Jeffrey Potash
Gazetteer of Vermont Heritage, published by The National Survey of Chester,
    Vermont
Hands on the Land: A History of the Vermont Landscape, by Jan Albers
*50 Hikes in Vermont: Walks, Hikes and Overnights in the Green Mountain State,
    Sixth Edition,* by the Green Mountain Club
Off the Leash: Subversive Journeys Around Vermont, by Helen Husher
Something Abides: Discovering the Civil War in Today's Vermont,
    by Howard Coffin
The Vermont Encyclopedia, by John J. Duffy, Samuel B. Hand, and Ralph H. Orth
The Vermont Ghost Guide, by Joseph A. Citro
The Vermont Quiz Book, by Melissa Lee Bryan and Frank Bryan
The Walker's Guide to Vermont, by the Green Mountain Club
Vermont Off the Beaten Path, 9th: A Guide to Unique Places, by Cindi D. Pietrzyk
Vermont Place Names: Footprints of History, by Esther Munroe Swift
Vermont Yearbook, published by The National Survey of Chester, Vermont

WEBSITES

251 Club of Vermont	vt251.com
Green Mountain Club	greenmountainclub.org
League of Local (Historical) Societies & Museums	vermonthistory.org
Roadside America: Vermont Attractions	roadsideamerica.com/location/vt
The Preservation Trust of Vermont	ptvermont.org
Vermont Life Magazine	vermontlife.com

VERMONT:

Agency of Transportation	vtrans.vermont.gov
Alliance of Independent Country Stores	vaics.org
Apple Orchards	vermontapples.org
Attractions Association	vtattractions.org
Brewers Association	vermontbrewers.com
Campgrounds Association	campvermont.com
Chamber of Commerce	vtchamber.com
Cheese Council	vtcheese.com
Covered Bridge Society	vermontbridges.com
Dairy	vermontdairy.com
Department of Forests, Parks & Recreation	vtfpr.org
Department of Libraries	libraries.vermont.gov
Fish & Wildlife Department	vtfishandwildlife.com
Fresh Network	vermontfresh.net
Hand Crafters	vermonthandcrafters.com
Historic Sites	historicsites.vermont.gov
Historical Society	vermonthistory.org
Information & Welcome Centers	bgs.vermont.gov/information_centers/ contact
Inn and Bed & Breakfast Association	vermontwaytostay.com
Maple Sugar Makers Association	vermontmaple.org
Old Cemetery Association	voca58.org
Outdoor Guide Association	voga.org
Ski Vermont	skivermont.com
State Parks	vtstateparks.com
Tourism & Marketing	vermontvacation.com
Working Farms	vermontfarms.org

VERMONT

From the Speech of

~ PRESIDENT CALVIN COOLIDGE ~

30th President of the United States

BENNINGTON, VERMONT, SEPTEMBER 21, 1928

"Vermont is a state I love. I could not look upon the peaks of Ascutney, Killington, Mansfield, and Equinox, without being moved in a way that no other scene could move me. It was here that I first saw the light of day; here I received my bride; here my dead lie, pillowed on the loving breast of our eternal hills.

I love Vermont because of her hills and valleys, her scenery and invigorating climate, but most of all because of her indomitable people. They are a race of pioneers who have almost beggared themselves to serve others. If the spirit of liberty should vanish in other parts of the Union, and support of our institutions should languish, it could all be replenished from the generous store held by the people of this brave little state of Vermont."

ADDISON ∼ *New Hampshire grant, 14 October 1761*

ALBANY ∼ *Vermont charter, 26 June 1782*

ALBURG ~ *Vermont charter, 23 February 1781*

ANDOVER ~ *New Hampshire grant, 13 October 1761*

ARLINGTON ~ *New Hampshire grant, 28 July 1761*

ATHENS ~ *Vermont charter, 3 May 1780*

AVERILL ～ *New Hampshire grant, 29 June 1762; an unorganized town*

AVERYS GORE ～ *Vermont charter, 27 January 1791*

BAKERSFIELD ∼ *Vermont charter, 25 January 1791*

BALTIMORE ∼ *Vermont act of incorporation, 19 October 1793*

BARNARD ~ *New Hampshire grant, 17 July 1761*

BARNET ~ *New Hampshire grant, 16 December 1763*

BARRE CITY ~ *Vermont act of incorporation, 23 November 1894*

BARTON ~ *Vermont charter, 20 October 1789*

BELVIDERE ~ *Vermont charter, 4 November 1791*

BENNINGTON ～ *New Hampshire grant, 3 January 1749*

BENSON ∼ *Vermont charter, 5 May 1780*

BERKSHIRE ∼ *Vermont charter, 22 June 1781*

Bethel in Vermont

I know a little town called Bethel,
   That good old Bible name:
East Bethel, Gilead and 'Lympus
   Of Mary E. Waller fame.

Of course you've heard of Bethel granite,
   A stone most beautiful,
Although it's not considered precious,
   It still is valuable.

But I would speak here of the town folk,
   No Bethelites of old
Could e'er have been more kindly gracious,
   Nor less aloof and cold.

So if afar, I should be lonely,
   Just pining by degrees,
I'd take the first train north and say,
   "I'll stop at Bethel please."

---May Clark McClellan

BERLIN ～ *New Hampshire grant, 8 June 1763*

BETHEL ～ *Vermont charter, 23 December 1779*

BLOOMFIELD ∼ *New Hampshire grant, 29 June 1762*

BOLTON ∼ *New Hampshire grant, 7 June 1763*

BRADFORD   *New York patent, 3 May 1770*

BRAINTREE   *Vermont chapter, 1 August 1781*

BRATTLEBORO ～ *New Hampshire grant, 26 December 1753*

BRIDGEWATER ～ *New Hampshire grant, 10 July 1761*

BRIDPORT ～ *New Hampshire grant, 9 October 1761*

BRIGHTON ~ *Vermont charter, 13 August 1781*

BRISTOL ~ *New Hampshire grant, 26 June 1762*

BROOKLINE ～ *Vermont act of incorporation, 30 November 1794*

BROWNINGTON ～ *Vermont charter, 2 October 1790*

BRUNSWICK ～ *New Hampshire grant, 13 October 1761*

BUELS GORE ～ *Vermont charter, 4 November 1780*

BURKE ~ *Vermont charter, 26 February 1782*

Island Point, Vt.

BURLINGTON ∼ *New Hampshire grant, 7 June 1763;*
incorporated as a city, 22 November 1864

CABOT ～ *Vermont charter, 17 August 1780*

CALAIS ～ *Vermont charter, 15 August 1781*

CAMBRIDGE ～ *Vermont charter, 30 August 1781*

CANAAN ∼ *Vermont charter, 25 February 1782*

CASTLETON ∼ *New Hampshire grant, 22 September 1761*

CAVENDISH ~ *New Hampshire grant, 12 October 1761*

CHARLESTON ~ *Vermont charter, 10 November 1780*

CHARLOTTE ～ *New Hampshire grant, 24 June 1762*

CHELSEA ～ *Vermont charter, 4 August 1781*

THE EDGE OF A VERMONT MAPLE SUGAR GROVE

CHITTENDEN ~ *Vermont charter, 16 March 1780*

CLARENDON ~ *New Hampshire grant, 5 September 1761*

COLCHESTER ～ *New Hampshire grant, 7 June 1763*

CONCORD ～ *Vermont charter, 15 September 1780*

CORINTH ～ *New Hampshire grant, 4 February 1764*

CORNWALL ~ *New Hampshire grant, 3 November 1761*

COVENTRY ~ *Vermont charter, 4 November 1780*

CRAFTSBURY ~ *Vermont charter, 23 August 1781*

DANBY ~ *New Hampshire grant, 27 August 1761*

DANVILLE ～ *Vermont charter, 31 October 1786*

Greetings from JOE'S POND, VT.

DERBY ∼ *Vermont charter, 29 October 1779*

DORSET ∼ *New Hampshire grant, 20 August 1761*

DOVER ~ *Vermont act of incorporation, 30 October 1810*

DUMMERSTON ~ *New Hampshire grant, 26 December 1753*

DUXBURY ～ *New Hampshire grant, 7 June 1763*

EAST HAVEN ～ *Vermont charter, 22 October 1790*

EAST MONTPELIER ∼ *Created by a Vermont legislative act, 1848*

EDEN ∼ *Vermont charter, 28 August 1781*

ELMORE ∼ *Vermont charter, 21 August 1781*

ENOSBURG ∼ *Vermont charter, 15 May 1780*

ESSEX ∾ *New Hampshire grant, 7 June 1763*

FAIRFAX ∽ *New Hampshire grant, 18 August 1763*

FAIRFIELD ∽ *New Hampshire grant, 18 August 1763*

FAIR HAVEN ~ *Vermont charter, 27 October 1779*

FAIRLEE ~ *New Hampshire grant, 9 September 1761*

FAYSTON ~ *Vermont charter of 27 February 1782*

FERDINAND ~ *New Hampshire grant, 12 October 1761;*
an unorganized town

FERRISBURGH ～ *New Hampshire grant, 24 June 1762*

FLETCHER ～ *Vermont charter, 20 August 1781*

FRANKLIN ～ *Vermont charter, 19 March 1789*

GEORGIA ～ *New Hampshire grant, 17 August 1763*

GLASTENBURY ～ *New Hampshire grant, 20 August 1761;*
unorganized, 1937

GLOVER ～ *Vermont charter, 20 November 1783*

GOSHEN ～ *Vermont charter, 2 February 1792*

GRAFTON ～ *New Hampshire grant, 8 April 1754*

GRANBY ～ *New Hampshire grant, 10 October 1761*

GRAND ISLE ～ *Vermont charter, 27 October 1779*

GRANVILLE ～ *Vermont charter, 2 August 1781*

GREENSBORO ～ *Vermont charter, 20 August 1781*

GROTON ~ *Vermont charter, 20 October 1789*

GUILDHALL ~ *New Hampshire grant, 10 October 1761*

GUILFORD ∾ *New Hampshire grant, 2 April 1754*

HALIFAX ∾ *New Hampshire grant, 11 May 1750*

HANCOCK ~ *Vermont charter, 31 July 1781*

HARDWICK ~ *Vermont charter, 19 August 1781*

HARTFORD ∾ *New Hampshire grant, 4 July 1761*

HARTLAND ~ *New Hampshire grant, 10 July 1761*

HIGHGATE ~ *New Hampshire grant, 17 August 1763*

HINESBURG ～ *New Hampshire grant, 24 June 1762*

HOLLAND ～ *Vermont charter, 26 October 1779*

HUBBARDTON ~ *New Hampshire grant, 15 June 1764*

HUNTINGTON ~ *New Hampshire grant, 7 June 1763*

HYDE PARK ～ *Vermont charter, 27 August 1781*

IRA ～ *Vermont charter, 9 November 1780*

IRASBURG ∼ *Vermont charter, 23 February 1781*

ISLE LA MOTTE ∼ *Vermont charter, 27 October 1779*

JAMAICA ～ *Vermont charter, 7 November 1780*

JAY ～ *Vermont charters, 7 November 1792 and 28 December 1792*

JERICHO ～ *New Hampshire grant, 7 June 1763*

JOHNSON ～ *Vermont charter, 2 January 1792*

KILLINGTON ~ *New Hampshire grant, 7 July 1761*

KIRBY ~ *Vermont act of incorporation, 28 October 1807*

LANDGROVE ∿ *Vermont charter, 9 November 1780*

LEICESTER ∿ *New Hampshire grant, 20 October 1761*

LEMINGTON ⟋ *New Hampshire grant, 29 June 1762*

LEWIS ⟋ *New Hampshire grant, 29 June 1762; an unorganized town*

LINCOLN ∾ *Vermont charter, 9 November 1780*

LONDONDERRY ∾ *Vermont charter, 20 April 1780*

LOWELL ～ *Vermont charter, 7 June 1791*

LUDLOW ～ *New Hampshire grant, 16 September 1761*

LUNENBURG ～ *New Hampshire grant, 5 July 1763*

LYNDON ～ *Vermont charter, 20 November 1780*

MAIDSTONE ～ *New Hampshire grant, 12 October 1761*

MANCHESTER ～ *New Hampshire grant, 11 August 1761*

MARLBORO ~ *New Hampshire grant, 29 April 1751*

MARSHFIELD ~ *Vermont legislative grant, 16 October 1782*

MIDDLEBURY ∾ *New Hampshire grant, 2 November 1761*

MIDDLESEX ～ *New Hampshire grant, 8 June 1763*

MIDDLETOWN SPRINGS ～ *Vermont act of incorporation,*
28 October 1784

MILTON ∽ *New Hampshire grant, 8 June 1763*

MONKTON ~ *New Hampshire grant, 24 June 1762*

MONTGOMERY ~ *Vermont charter, 8 October 1789*

MONTPELIER ～ *Vermont town charter, 14 August 1781; incorporated as a city, 5 March 1895*

Vermont is called "Green Mountain State"
For worth and wealth we deem her great,
Her emblem clover doth exhale
Perfume from each hill and vale.

RED CLOVER
VERMONT STATE
FLOWER

STATE CAPITOL, MONTPELIER, VERMONT.

MORETOWN ～ *New Hampshire grant, 7 June 1763*

MORGAN ～ *Vermont charter, 6 November 1780*

MORRISTOWN ～ *Vermont charter, 24 August 1781*

MOUNT HOLLY ~ *Vermont act of incorporation, 31 October 1792*

MOUNT TABOR ~ *New Hampshire grant, 28 August 1761*

NEWARK ~ *Vermont charter, 15 August 1781*

NEWBURY ~ *New Hampshire grant, 18 May 1763*

NEWFANE ～ *New Hampshire grant, 19 June 1753*

NEW HAVEN ～ *New Hampshire grant, 2 November 1761*

NEWPORT CITY ～ *Incorporated as a city in 1917*

Moonlight on Lake Memphremagog, Vermont.

NEWPORT TOWN ～ *Vermont charter, 30 October 1802*

NORTHFIELD ～ *Vermont charter, 10 August 1781*

NORTH HERO ~ *Vermont charter, 27 October 1779*

NORTON ~ *Vermont charter, 26 October 1779*

NORWICH ～ *New Hampshire grant, 4 July 1761*

ORANGE ～ *Vermont charter, 11 August 1781*

ORWELL ～ *New Hampshire grant, 18 August 1763*

PANTON ～ *New Hampshire grant, 3 November 1761*

PAWLET ～ *New Hampshire grant, 26 August 1761*

PEACHAM ～ *New Hampshire grant, 31 December 1763*

PERU ~ *New Hampshire grant, 13 October 1761*

PITTSFIELD ~ *Vermont charter of 29 July 1781*

PITTSFORD ～ *New Hampshire grant, 12 October 1761*

PLAINFIELD ～ *Vermont act of incorporation, 10 November 1797*

PLYMOUTH ～ *New Hampshire grant, 6 July 1761*

POMFRET ～ *New Hampshire grant, 8 July 1761*

POULTNEY ⁓ *New Hampshire grant, 21 September 1761*

POWNAL ⁓ *New Hampshire grant, 8 January 1760*

PROCTOR ～ *Vermont act of incorporation, 18 November 1886*

PUTNEY ～ *New Hampshire grant, 26 December 1753*

READING ~ *New Hampshire grant, 6 June 1761*

READSBORO ~ *New York patent, 24 April 1770*

RICHFORD ~ *Vermont charter, 21 August 1780*

RICHMOND ~ *Vermont act of incorporation, 27 October 1794*

RIPTON ～ *Vermont charter, 13 April 1781*

ROCHESTER ～ *Vermont charter, 30 July 1781*

ROCKINGHAM ～ *New Hampshire grant, 28 December 1752*

ROXBURY ～ *Vermont charter, 6 August 1781*

ROYALTON ~ *New York patent, 13 November 1769*

RUPERT ~ *New Hampshire grant, 20 August 1761*

Rutland, Vt. Center Street.

The Girls here in Rutland are so sweet and entertaining that after a short visit one can hardly bear to leave the place.

RUTLAND TOWN ~ *New Hampshire grant, 7 September 1761*

RYEGATE ~ *New Hampshire grant, 8 September 1763*

ST. ALBANS CITY ~ *Originally part of St Albans Town,*
New Hampshire grant, 17 August 1763.
Incorporated as a village, 18 November 1859 and
as a city, 3 March 1902

ST. ALBANS TOWN ~ *New Hampshire grant, 17 August 1763*

ST. GEORGE ~ *New Hampshire grant, 18 August 1763*

SALISBURY ~ *New Hampshire grant, 3 November 1761*

SANDGATE ~ *New Hampshire grant, 11 August 1761*

SEARSBURG ∼ *Vermont charter, 23 February 1781*

SHAFTSBURY ∼ *New Hampshire grant, 20 August 1761*

SHARON ~ *New Hampshire grant, 17 August 1761*

SHEFFIELD ~ *Vermont charter, 25 October 1793*

SHELBURNE ～ *New Hampshire grant, 18 August 1763*

SHELDON ∾ *New Hampshire grant, 18 August 1763*

SHOREHAM ∾ *New Hampshire grant, 8 October 1761*

SHREWSBURY ~ *New Hampshire grant, 4 September 1761*

SOMERSET ~ *New Hampshire grant, 9 September 1761;*
unorganized, 1937

SOUTH BURLINGTON

Originally incorporated as a separate town, 22 November 1864; incorporated as a city, 1971

Camel's Hump, Vermont

9334

SPRINGFIELD ~ *New Hampshire grant, 20 August 1761*

STAMFORD ～ *New Hampshire grant, 6 March 1753*

STANNARD ～ *Vermont act of incorporation, 19 August 1867*

STARKSBORO ∽ *Vermont charter, 9 November 1780*

STOCKBRIDGE ∽ *New Hampshire grant, 21 July 1761*

STOWE ~ *New Hampshire grant, 8 June 1763*

STRAFFORD ~ *New Hampshire grant, 12 August 1761*

STRATTON ~ *New Hampshire grant, 30 July 1761*

SUDBURY ~ *New Hampshire grant, 6 August 1763*

SUNDERLAND ~ *New Hampshire grant, 29 July 1761*

SUTTON ~ *Vermont charter, 26 February 1782*

SWANTON ～ *New Hampshire grant, 17 August 1763*

THETFORD ～ *New Hampshire grant, 12 August 1761*

TINMOUTH ～ *New Hampshire grant, 15 September 1761*

TOPSHAM ～ *New Hampshire grant, 17 August 1763*

TOWNSHEND ~ *New Hampshire grant, 20 June 1753*

TROY ~ *Vermont charter, 28 October 1801*

Dear Maude.
Would it be
to much

Series 70
Hartman & Co., Boston, Mass.
M. Janes, Richford, Vt.

Post Card

This side may be used for correspondence.

This side for address only.

trouble to try and get
three yds Black Val Lace
not over one inch wide
And two yds Black
insertion to match
about the same width
I can't get it any where in
Richford. Got your postal
this morning will be glad
to see you. With love from
all, to you and Will.
From Mary.

Mrs Maude Fauchs.

North Try.

Vermont.

VERGENNES ∿ *Vermont charter, 23 October 1788*

VERNON ~ *Massachusetts grant of 1672*

VERSHIRE ~ *Vermont charter, 3 August 1781*

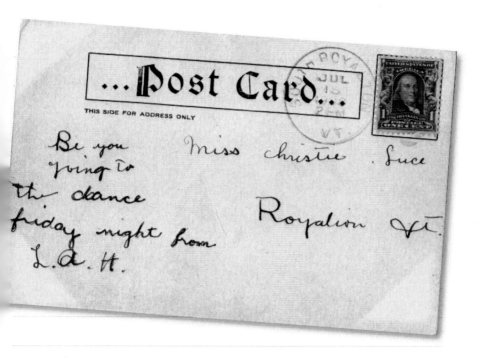

Be you
going to
the dance
friday night from
L. a. H.

Miss Christie . Luce

Royalton Vt.

WALDEN ∼ *Vermont charter, 18 August 1781*

WALLINGFORD ∼ *New Hampshire grant, 27 November 1761*

WALTHAM ～ *Vermont act of incorporation, 31 October 1796*

WARDSBORO ～ *Vermont charter, 7 November 1780*

WARNERS GRANT ∼ *Vermont charter, 29 November 1791*

WARREN ∼ *Vermont legislative grant, 9 November 1780*

WARREN GORE ∾ *Vermont charter, 20 October 1789*

WASHINGTON ∾ *Vermont charter, 8 August 1781*

WATERBURY ～ *New Hampshire grant, 7 June 1763*

WATERFORD ～ *Vermont charter, 8 November 1780*

WATERVILLE ～ *Vermont act of incorporation, 15 November 1824*

WEATHERSFIELD ～ *New Hampshire grant, 20 August 1761*

WELLS ~ *New Hampshire grant, 15 September 1761*

WEST FAIRLEE ~ *Vermont act of incorporation, 25 February 1797*

WESTFIELD ~ *Vermont charter, 15 May 1780*

WESTFORD ~ *New Hampshire grant, 8 June 1763*

WEST HAVEN ～ *Vermont act of incorporation, 20 October 1792*

WESTMINSTER ～ *New Hampshire grant, 9 November 1752*

WESTMORE ∼ *Vermont charter, 17 August 1781*

WEST RUTLAND ∼ *Vermont act of incorporation, 19 November 1886*

WEST WINDSOR ∼ *Vermont act of incorporation, 26 October 1848*

WESTON ∼ *Vermont act of incorporation, 26 October 1799*

THIS SPACE FOR WRITING MESSAGES

What do you
think of our
school, some
place, believe
me, I wish I
was on the
good old farm
again, and that
classy music we
had. Mae.

MADE IN GERMANY

252.-6129

POST CARD

THIS SPACE FOR ADDRESS ONLY

U.S. POSTAGE
ONE CENT

RUTLAND
SEP 7
1235PM
VT

Mr. Leo Lovell,
Bellows Falls,
Vermont

WHEELOCK ~ *Vermont charter, 14 June 1785*

WHITING ~ *New Hampshire grant, 6 August 1763*

WHITINGHAM ~ *New York patent, 12 March 1770*

WILLIAMSTOWN ~ *Vermont charter, 9 August 1781*

WILLISTON ~ *New Hampshire grant, 7 June 1763*

WILMINGTON ～ *New Hampshire grant, 29 April 1751*

WINDHAM ～ *Vermont act of incorporation, 22 October 1795*

WINDSOR ~ *New Hampshire grant, 6 July 1761*

WINHALL ~ *New Hampshire grant, 15 September 1761*

WINOOSKI ∼ *Incorporated as a city, 1 April 1921*

WOLCOTT ～ *Vermont charter, 22 August 1781*

WOODBURY ～ *Vermont charter, 16 August 1781*

WOODFORD ～ *New Hampshire grant, 6 March 1753*

In January, 1934, on this pasture hill of Clinton Gilbert's farm, an endless-rope tow, powered by a Model "T" Ford engine, hauled skiers uphill for the first time. This ingenious contraption launched a new era in winter sports.

WOODSTOCK ～ *New Hampshire grant, 10 July 1761*

WORCESTER ～ *New Hampshire grant, 8 June 1763*

RATES OF TOLL

	CENTS
A FOUR WHEELED PLEASURE CARRIAGE DRAWN BY TWO BEASTS _ _ _ _	50
EACH ADDITIONAL BEAST _ _ _ _ _ _	4
A TWO WHEELED PLEASURE CARRIAGE DRAWN BY ONE BEAST_ _ _ _ _	25
EACH ADDITIONAL BEAST _ _ _ _ _	4
A WAGON DRAWN BY TWO BEASTS _ _	25
EACH ADDITIONAL BEAST _ _ _ _ _	4
A HORSE WAGON DRAWN BY ONE BEAST	20
EACH ADDITIONAL BEAST _ _ _ _ _	4
A CART DRAWN BY TWO OXEN _ _ _ _	20
EACH ADDITIONAL BEAST _ _ _ _ _	3
A PLEASURE SLEIGH DRAWN BY TWO HORSES	20
A PLEASURE SLEIGH DRAWN BY ONE HORSE	12
A SLED OR LUMBER SLEIGH DRAWN BY TWO BEASTS _ _ _ _ _ _	12
A SLED OR LUMBER SLEIGH DRAWN BY ONE HORSE _ _ _ _ _	8
EACH HORSE AND RIDER _ _ _ _ _	6
ALL HORSES MULES OR NEAT CATTLE _	2 CENTS EACH
ALL SHEEP OR SWINE AT THE RATE OF _	6 CENTS A DOZEN